AUTHOR'S NOTE:

Humans have always been fascinated by space. In the sixteenth century, Nicolaus Copernicus first suggested that Earth and the planets revolved around the Sun. It took several centuries and the work of astronomers, like Johannes Kepler and Galileo Galilei, before it was accepted as fact. The pace of space exploration has picked up a bit since then.

Since the middle of the twentieth century, humanity has launched the first satellite into orbit, sent men to the Moon, landed rovers on Mars, and there is still so much left to explore.

I'd like to thank the pioneering work of the scientists, engineers, and educators who made it possible for me to research a book about outer space from the comfort of my home here on Earth. Because, as you're about to find out, space is not known for its hospitality.

Special thanks to Dr. Jacqueline Faherty of the American Museum of Natural History for her expert review of the material.

For Alex. Space pants!

The Goldilocks Zone • Copyright © 2021 by Drew Sheneman • All rights reserved. Manufactured in Italy • No part of this book may be used or reproduced in any manner whatsoever without written permission except in the case of brief quotations embodied in critical articles and reviews • For information address HarperCollins Children's Books, a division of HarperCollins Publishers, 195 Broadway, New York, NY 10007. www.harpercollinschildrens.com • Library of Congress Control Number: 2020911620 • ISBN 978-0-06-297236-1. Design by Drew Sheneman and Chelsea C. Donaldson • 21 22 23 24 RTLO 10 9 8 7 6 5 4 3 2 1 ❖ First Edition

THE GOLDILOCKS ZONE

BY DREW SHENEMAN

REAL FACTS ABOUT OUTER SPACE

HARPER

An Imprint of HarperCollinsPublishers

This is our solar system, a small neighborhood-sized
chunk of the universe with our Sun at the center.
There are seven other planets in our solar system, but
only one Earth.

NEPTUNE

SATURN

URANUS

JUPITER

Our place in the solar system is what makes Earth such a great home. It's not too close to the Sun and not too far away.

Scientists call this
THE GOLDILOCKS ZONE.

It's called the Goldilocks Zone because Earth is the only planet in the solar system that isn't too hot or too cold for life to thrive.

That's right. If you don't believe me, ask a scientist.

First stop . . . Mercury!

Mercury is the smallest planet in the solar system. It's also the closest to the Sun. At an average of just 48 million miles from Earth, Mercury is practically just around the corner.

The funny thing is that while the parts of Mercury facing the Sun are extremely hot (about 800 degrees Fahrenheit) . . .

the parts facing away from the sun are incredibly cold (about -300 degrees Fahrenheit).

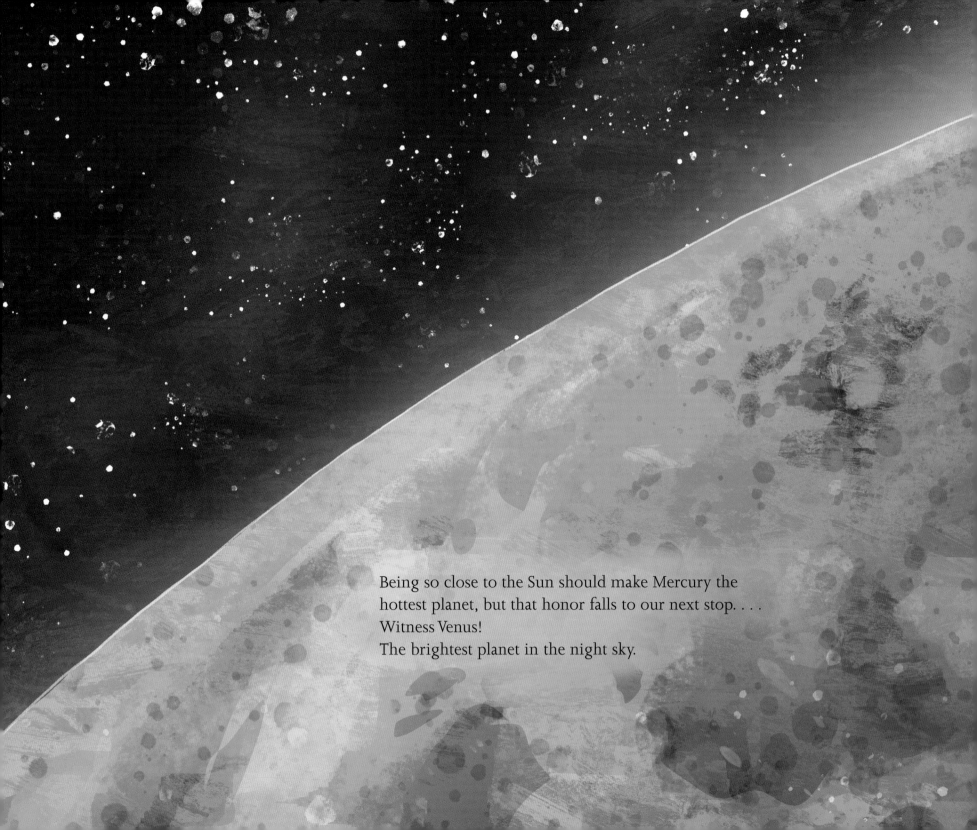

Being so close to the Sun should make Mercury the
hottest planet, but that honor falls to our next stop. . . .
Witness Venus!
The brightest planet in the night sky.

Venus is so hot because its thick atmosphere traps the heat from the Sun. Scientists have sent probes to Venus, but they only lasted, at most, a few hours before their electronics failed.

THE VENERA 7, A SOVIET SPACE PROBE, LANDED ON VENUS IN 1970.

OUT OF ORDER

If that wasn't bad enough, the air on Venus is poisonous, the lightning is frequent, and the pressure on the surface would crush you.

VENUS IS A BUMMER!

After Venus, the next stop from the Sun is Earth and then Mars.

MERCURY:
36 MILLION MILES
FROM THE SUN

Over the years, we have sent a number of robotic rovers to explore the surface of Mars.

While scientists haven't discovered any life on the planet, they did discover water underneath the Martian surface. Despite no sign of life today, there may have been some form of life on Mars millions or billions of years ago.

Of all the planets other than Earth, Mars would be the most livable for humans. But if we ever attempt to live on Mars, we will have to bring food, shelter, water, and even air with us.

If you ever traveled to Jupiter, you couldn't even stand on the surface because it does not have a surface to stand on. The planet is just a big, slushy ball of gas and ice, which grows thicker down to its core.

LIKE THE WORST SLURPEE IN THE UNIVERSE.

Jupiter is more massive than all the other planets in the solar system combined. Jupiter is so massive and its gravity so strong that it affects the fate of the other planets.

Billions of years ago, when the solar system was still forming, Jupiter started drifting closer to the Sun. When it did, Jupiter's powerful gravity may have dislodged a rock from the asteroid belt between it and Mars. Some scientists think that may have been the asteroid that hit Earth and killed the nonavian dinosaurs.

Nearly 403 million miles further out in space is the ringed planet of Saturn. If you tried to drive there from Jupiter, it would take 279,861 days, assuming you observed Earth speed limits.

WE'RE STILL NOT THERE—AND I STILL HAVE TO PEE.

Saturn's stunning rings are made of trillions of chunks of ice.

If you tried to stand on the surface of Saturn, you'd sink into a toxic soup of gas and ice until the pressure popped you like a grape.

Our next stop is Uranus. This planet might have a funny name, but you do not want to live here.

Uranus and Neptune are a lot like Jupiter and Saturn, but colder.

Both are also made of gas, but much of that gas is frozen, so scientists also call them ice giants.

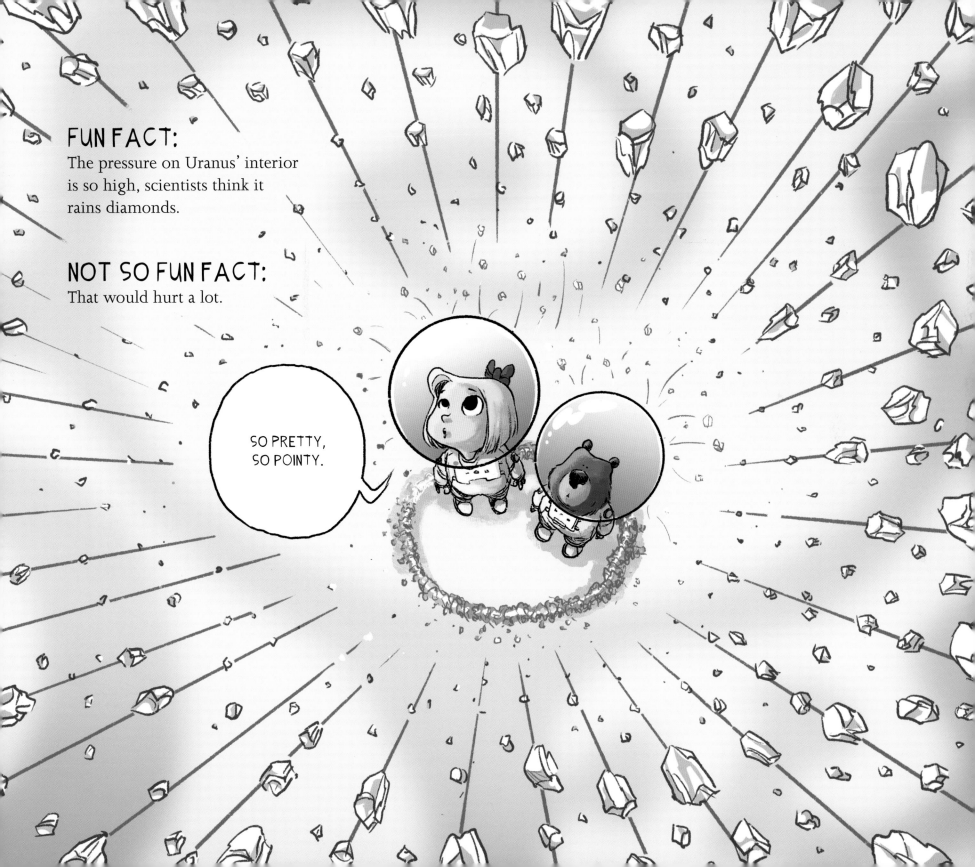

NEARLY ONE BILLION MILES FURTHER OUT IN SPACE IS NEPTUNE, THE BLUE PLANET.

The temperature on Neptune is a brisk 392 degrees Fahrenheit below zero.

Neptune also has the strongest storms in the solar system with winds traveling 1200 miles per hour. That is faster than a fighter jet.

Neptune's atmosphere is made of hydrogen, helium, and methane. The methane is what gives it that vibrant blue color.

Far beyond the planets and the Kuiper Belt, a ring of comets, asteroids, and icy bodies, lies Pluto. Pluto was once considered a planet.

To qualify for planetary status, an object must do three things:

1. ORBIT A STAR LIKE THE SUN
2. HAVE ENOUGH MASS TO MAINTAIN A ROUND SHAPE
3. CLEAR ITS ORBIT OF OTHER OBJECTS

Pluto does the first two, but not the third, therefore Pluto is not a planet.

You know what else aren't planets? The Sun and Moon.

The Sun is a star. It provides Earth with the heat and light we need to live. Any closer would be too hot, any farther away too cold.

Earth has it all!
Food! Air! Water!
And temperatures that won't
cause you to burst into flames.

There is life in every nook and cranny of Earth.

From the depths of the ocean . . .

to the tops of the highest mountains . . .

Life on Earth is diverse,
and it is everywhere!

Not necessarily. The universe is an awful big place, and we have only explored a tiny piece of it. It's possible that somewhere out there, another planet is just the right place for life to thrive.

But we only have one Earth for now, so let's do our best to take care of it.

PLANET

JUPITER:
NAMED AFTER THE ROMAN KING OF GODS

VENUS:
CLOSEST IN SIZE, MASS, AND DENSITY TO EARTH

NEPTUNE:
ONE YEAR ON NEPTUNE IS EQUAL TO NEARLY 165 EARTH YEARS

MARS:
THE TALLEST MOUNTAIN ON MARS IS 16 MILES HIGH, ABOUT TWO AND A HALF TIMES HIGHER THAN MOUNT EVEREST

FACTS

URANUS:

HAS RINGS LIKE SATURN, BUT THEY ARE OLDER AND COVERED IN SPACE DUST, THUS HARDER TO SEE

MERCURY:

ORBITS THE SUN ONCE EVERY 88 DAYS

SATURN:

HAS 53 KNOWN MOONS WITH ANOTHER 29 AWAITING CONFIRMATION

EARTH:

HOME OF THE SOLAR SYSTEM'S LARGEST BALL OF TWINE